Who Are You?

Enneagram

Virginia Loh-Hagan

45TH PARALLEL PRESS

Published in the United States of America by Cherry Lake Publishing Group
Ann Arbor, Michigan
www.cherrylakepublishing.com

Reading Adviser: Marla Conn, MS, Ed., Literacy specialist, Read-Ability, Inc.
Book Designer: Felicia Macheske

Photo Credits: © rui vale sousa/Shutterstock.com, cover; © Dan Kosmayer/Shutterstock.com, cover; © GzP_Design/Shutterstock.com, cover;© Monkey Business Images/Shutterstock.com, 5, 27; © igorstevanovic/Shutterstock.com, 6; © Finchen/Shutterstock.com, 9; © May_Chanikran/Shutterstock.com, 11; © SaMBa/Shutterstock.com, 12; © Samuel Borges Photography/Shutterstock.com, 14; © Donna Ellen Coleman/Shutterstock.com, 17; © PetraGodart/Shutterstock.com, 18; © Rawpixel.com/Shutterstock.com, 20; © StunningArt/Shutterstock.com, 22; © Prostock-studio/Shutterstock.com, 25; © otnaydur/Shutterstock.com, 29

Graphics Throughout: © AKaiser/Shutterstock.com; © galastudio/Shutterstock.com; © tanyabosyk/Shutterstock.com; © ViSnezh/Shutterstock.com; © MARINA ARABADZHI/Shutterstock.com; © Alisa Burkovska/Shutterstock.com

45th Parallel Press is an imprint of Cherry Lake Publishing Group.

Library of Congress Cataloging-in-Publication Data

Names: Loh-Hagan, Virginia, author.
Title: Enneagram / by Virginia Loh-Hagan.
Description: Ann Arbor, Michigan : Cherry Lake Publishing, [2020]
| Series: Who are you? | Includes index.
Identifiers: LCCN 2020006893 (print) | LCCN 2020006894 (ebook)
| ISBN 9781534169142 (hardcover) | ISBN 9781534170827 (paperback)
| ISBN 9781534172661 (pdf) | ISBN 9781534174504 (ebook)
Subjects: LCSH: Enneagram—Juvenile literature. | Personality tests—Juvenile literature.
Classification: LCC BF698.35.E54 L64 2020 (print) | LCC BF698.35.E54 (ebook) | DDC 155.2/6—dc23
LC record available at https://lccn.loc.gov/2020006893
LC ebook record available at https://lccn.loc.gov/2020006894

Cherry Lake Publishing Group would like to acknowledge the work of the Partnership for 21st Century Learning, a Network of Battelle for Kids. Please visit *http://www.battelleforkids.org/networks/p21* for more information.

Printed in the United States of America
Corporate Graphics

Dr. Virginia Loh-Hagan is an author, university professor, and former classroom teacher. She took a free online Enneagram Personality Test (www.truity.com). Her primary type is "The Achiever," which makes sense. She lives in San Diego, California, with her very tall husband and very naughty dogs. To learn more about her, visit www.virginialoh.com.

Chapter One

Living Fully and Freely

What is the Enneagram?

What is the Enneagram shape?

The **Enneagram** is a personality typing system. It shows people how their emotions affect their lives. It also shows how people relate to others. All people want things. All people need things. But people want and need different things. Each Enneagram personality type has a certain way of seeing the world. The Enneagram personality system attempts to explain why people act in certain ways.

Some people use their Enneagram type to help themselves. They want to lead a better life. First, they learn about their type. Then they think about how they adapt and respond to different events. Next, they work on improving themselves. They also work on understanding other people. They work on living fully and freely.

Find a free online Enneagram test.
What is your Enneagram type?

Enneagram is a combination of two Greek words. *Ennea* means "9." *Gramma* means "drawn or written." An enneagram is actually a geometric shape. It looks like a 9-pointed star. The personality system is named after this shape.

The Enneagram system has 9 personality types. Each type is mapped on a circle with 9 points. The circle is the unity of human life. Each point represents a personality type. Each person has a **core** type. Core means main. Each person also has 2 **wing** types. Wings are related personality types. They're the numbers before or after the core type.

Who is your true self? Finding your type is not the end point. It's the beginning of a journey of self-discovery.

FUN FACTS

- The Enneagram is often used in businesses. It's used as a tool to help people work together as a team. It helps people become better leaders. It helps people become better people.

- Sleeping At Last is a band. In 2019, they made an album called *Atlas: Enneagram*. This album has 9 songs. Each song is about each of the 9 Enneagram types.

- Enneagram has become very popular. People pay for "Enneagram coaches." They pay a lot of money for self-help sessions. They also pay a lot of money to train to become coaches.

- Enneagram has been called a "fake science." Some scientists think the Enneagram tests are more like horoscopes than personality tests.

Lines are drawn inside the circle. These lines connect the points. They show how people are divided. They also show how the types relate to each other. Each core type has connecting lines that lead to another type. One line could go to the personality type someone uses to deal with stress. Another line could go to the type someone uses to grow. This means the Enneagram is **dynamic**. Dynamic means being able to change. People change their personality types.

The connecting lines meet at certain points. Some Enneagram experts think these points are also important to understanding personalities.

Study the Enneagram. What other shapes do you see? Why are these shapes important?

Chapter Two

From Mystical Origins

Who is George Ivanovitch Gurdjieff? Who is Oscar Ichazo? Who is Claudio Naranjo?

No one knows how the Enneagram really started. Some experts think it started 4,500 years ago in Babylonia. (Today, Babylonia is Iraq.) Other experts think it started 2,500 years ago in **ancient** Greece. Ancient means from a long time ago.

Today's Enneagram **symbol** was developed by George Ivanovitch Gurdjieff. A symbol is a picture or sign. Gurdjieff was born in Armenia around 1870. He was a **mystic**. Mystics practice deep thought or prayer. Gurdjieff believed people lived in a "waking sleep." He wanted people to awaken to a higher state of being. He created the Enneagram symbol. This happened in the 1930s. His symbol represented never-ending motion.

Enneagram is best explored while practicing meditation. Meditation is the act of reflecting. Yoga is a form of meditation. It has special movements. How do you meditate?

Oscar Ichazo was born in 1931. He's from Bolivia. He used Gurdjieff's symbol. He traveled a lot. He picked up many ideas. He developed the 9 personality types. He created the term "Enneagram of Personality." He made the Enneagram popular in the 1960s.

Ichazo's Enneagram system comes from many ancient sources. It uses ideas from Judaism, Christianity, Islam, Buddhism, and the ancient Greeks. One of Ichazo's main sources was the Desert Fathers. The Desert Fathers were early Christian mystics. They lived in ancient Egypt. They believed in the "7 deadly sins." Seven of the 9 Enneagram types are connected to these sins. Ichazo also used the Jewish idea of the "tree of life." This is a map of God's laws for all creation.

Some experts connect the Enneagram symbol to ancient Greek geometry. What do you know about geometry?

EXPLAINED BY

SCIENCE

People have many fears. But each person fears different things in different ways. Each Enneagram type has a different basic fear. For example, Type 2 fears being unloved. Type 2 spends more time than others to avoid this fear. Fear is a natural response. It's needed for survival. Fear is a chain reaction. It starts with a scare. This scare sends signals to the brain. The brain sends messages to different body parts. The body feels stress. It will react. The heart will race. Breathing will become fast and quick. The body will figure out if it's in danger. It wants to protect itself. Other senses kick in. Ears will listen for danger. Eyes will look for danger. This information is sent to the brain as well. Specifically, it's sent to the hypothalamus. This part of the brain determines if you should fight or flee.

Claudio Naranjo lived from 1932 to 2019. He was from Chile. He was a **psychiatrist**. Psychiatrists are medical doctors. They study how the mind works. Naranjo learned about the Enneagram from Ichazo. He added more medical terms to Ichazo's model. He made the types clearer.

At first, the Enneagram was only taught to a select few. Only small groups of people were allowed to learn it. But then word got out. More and more people believed in it. Schools and communities grew around the Enneagram. Some Jewish and Christian priests adapted the Enneagram into their synagogues and churches.

Books were written about the Enneagram. It became popular in the United States in the 1970s.

Read a book or a blog about the Enneagram.
What more did you learn?

Chapter Three

Nine Personality Types

What are the 9 personality types of the Enneagram? What is a tritype?

The Enneagram has 9 personality types. Type 1 is "The **Reformer**." A reformer is a person who changes things. Type 1 people want to improve the world. They have a strong sense of right and wrong. They hate making mistakes. They want things to be perfect. But they can be stubborn.

Type 2 is "The Helper." These people are giving. They take care of others. They want to be loved. But they may forget to take care of themselves.

Type 3 is "The Achiever." These people want to be successful. They're good presenters. They strive to be the best. They like to compete. They want to win. But they may work too much. They may be hard to please.

Each type has strengths. Each has weaknesses. Each has opportunities for growth. What are your strengths, weaknesses, and growth opportunities?

Type 4 is "The Individualist." These people are self-aware. They're creative. They tend to be artists. They like to do things their own way. They strive to be special. But they may have a hard time connecting.

Type 5 is "The Investigator." These people are curious. They see things in different ways. They like to learn things. They're good inventors. They're good explorers. They may go off on their own. But they may often not think before they act.

Type 6 is "The Loyalist." These people are responsible. They're hard workers. They protect themselves and others. But they may have a hard time trusting. They may be fearful.

Read more about each type. What are some areas of improvement for each number type?

Type 7 is "The **Enthusiast**." Enthusiasm means having a lot of energy. These people like having fun. They're playful. They're social. They want to experience new things. They keep busy. They're very active. But they can also be easily distracted.

Type 8 is "The **Challenger**." Challengers question things. These people are confident. They take charge. They're great leaders. They can be **rebels**. Rebels break rules. At times, Type 8 people may not be the best team players.

Type 9 is "The Peacemaker." These people support others. They're easy to get along with. They're friendly. They're positive. They avoid anything negative. But they may also have a hard time making decisions.

Think about examples from your life.
How are you like each of these types?

REAL-LIFE CONNECTION

The Enneagram is on Instagram! Many people are posting their Enneagram types as a hashtag. People are becoming famous because of their Enneagram posts. For example, Christina Wilcox has over 115,000 followers. She lives in Dallas, Texas. She's an illustrator. She shares art about the 9 Enneagram types. She said, "I don't feel like I'm positioning myself as an Enneagram expert. I'm someone who is using their creativity to help others express themselves through their Enneagram type."

Sarajane Case is a Type 7. She also has a popular Enneagram Instagram account. Her online content is called "Enneagram & Coffee." She has over 577,000 followers. She shares tips and fun memes. She said, "The Enneagram is my chosen tool for working with myself and others to know who they are, how they operate, and what might get in the way of their deepest desires." Case also has a blog and podcast.

A person's overall personality consists of 3 Enneagram types. This is called a **tritype**. A person's tritype has 3 numbers. The first number is the core type. The second and third numbers are types chosen from each of the other **triads**. They're ranked in order of preference. Triads are groups of 3. The triads are below:

- The Heart triad focuses on feeling. How would you avoid shame? How would you establish self-image? Depending on your answers, you'd be Type 2, 3, or 4.
- The Head triad focuses on thinking. How would you avoid fear? How would you feel safe and manage stress? Depending on your answers, you'd be Type 5, 6, or 7.
- The Belly triad focuses on **instinct**. Instincts are gut feelings. How would you avoid anger? How would you create boundaries? Depending on your answers, you'd be Type 8, 9, or 1.

Katherine and David Fauvre developed the tritype system from Ichazo's ideas. Learn more about it. What is your tritype?

Chapter Four

Famous Examples

What is Oprah Winfrey's Enneagram? How are Dr. Martin Luther King Jr. and Joseph Stalin connected? What traits do Eleanor Roosevelt and Queen Elizabeth II share?

Oprah Winfrey was the richest African American of the 20th century. Some experts think Winfrey is a 3w2. This means her core personality is Type 3 and her wing is Type 2. Her core personality type shows up in her success. She has her own media empire. Winfrey's wing type shows up in her generosity. She gives away a lot of money. She helps her communities.

Some experts think Winfrey's tritype is 369. Type 3 is her core personality. Self-image is important to her. She wants to be the best. Type 6 explains her work **ethic**. Ethics are rules of behavior. She works hard. She feels safe by ensuring her place in the world. She protects her reputation. Last is Type 9. She avoids anger by being charming and friendly. Her fans make her feel important.

People use all 3 of their tritype personality types. They use them to succeed. They use them to solve problems. How will you use your tritype?

Each Enneagram type shows up in 3 ways. One way is healthy, or good. Another way is **average**. Average means in the middle. It's not good or bad. The last way is unhealthy, or bad.

Dr. Martin Luther King Jr. and Joseph Stalin were both Type 8 personalities. King was a civil rights leader. He fought for justice. He wanted African Americans to have freedoms. He believed in nonviolent protests. He used his personality traits in a healthy way.

Stalin was the leader of the USSR (now Russia). Millions of people died under his rule. He ruled by terror. He killed anyone who disagreed with him. He used his personality traits in an unhealthy way.

How we use our personality matters.
Are you healthy, average, or unhealthy?

SPOTLIGHT

BIOGRAPHY

Richard Rohr is an American author. He is a Type 1. He was born in 1943 in Kansas. A group of Rohr's colleagues went to Chile. They studied under Oscar Ichazo. They went back to the United States. They taught others. They shared what they learned by word of mouth. Rohr was one of the students. He helped make Enneagram popular in the United States. He wrote a book about the Enneagram in 1990. It's called *The Enneagram: A Christian Perspective*. Rohr recorded one of his teaching sessions about the Enneagram. Many people listened to his recordings. He's known for introducing American Christians to the Enneagram. Rohr wrote in the book, "The Enneagram's purpose is to help us uncover the traps that keep us from living fully and freely as our true self so that we will use our unique, authentic gifts for the good of others and the world."

Determining personalities is hard. For example, Type 2 and Type 9 are similar. Both types focus on connecting with people. (Average Type 9 people are often mistaken for healthy Type 2.) But there are differences. Type 9 people are won over by the ideal versions of people. Type 2 people are more aware of people's true selves.

Both Eleanor Roosevelt and Queen Elizabeth II served others. But they served in different ways. Roosevelt was a Type 2. She was a **first lady** of the United States. The first lady is the wife of a U.S. president. She made life better for many people. She did many community projects. Elizabeth II is the longest ruling queen of England. She's a Type 9. She believes in duty. She works hard to keep the peace.

You might see yourself in different types. Read more about the types. What are the differences between the types?

WHO ARE YOU?

TAKE THE QUIZ!

What is your greatest fear? Each Enneagram type has a core fear. People work hard to avoid their fears.

- You fear doing evil: **Type 1**
- You fear being unloved: **Type 2**
- You fear failure: **Type 3**
- You fear not having a life purpose: **Type 4**
- You fear being useless or helpless: **Type 5**
- You fear not having rules: **Type 6**
- You fear missing out: **Type 7**
- You fear being controlled by others: **Type 8**
- You fear war and conflicts: **Type 9**

Which fictional character are you more like? These characters embody certain Enneagram types.

- Hermione Granger from the Harry Potter series. She likes to get things right: **Type 1**
- Sam Gamgee from the Lord of the Rings series. He supports his friends. He never loses hope: **Type 2**
- Iron Man. Iron Man is successful. He avoids failure: **Type 3**
- Anne Shirley from the Anne of Green Gables series. She has a great imagination: **Type 4**
- Sherlock Holmes. He is really smart and knows it. He notices everything: **Type 5**
- The White Rabbit from *Alice's Adventures in Wonderland*. He sees danger everywhere. But he's loyal: **Type 6**
- Peter Pan. He loves adventures. He lives life to the fullest: **Type 7**
- Jo March from *Little Women*. She rebels against what society says she can and can't do: **Type 8**
- Dorothy from *The Wizard of Oz*. She wants everyone to be happy. She makes friends easily: **Type 9**

DISCLAIMER: All the quizzes and questions in this book are designed for entertainment purposes only. They shouldn't be used as advice. They shouldn't be taken seriously. There is no guarantee of accuracy. But they're fun! To download a copy of this quiz, please visit: https://cherrylakepublishing.com/teaching_guides.

How do you talk? Enneagram types have different speaking styles.

- You use precise language. You share a lot of details: **Type 1**
- You like to give advice. You say nice things: **Type 2**
- You motivate others. You use a lot of hand gestures: **Type 3**
- You have a calm voice. You share your opinions: **Type 4**
- You don't like to chat. You get right to the point: **Type 5**
- You ask serious questions. You like to see all sides: **Type 6**
- You're entertaining. You focus on the positive: **Type 7**
- You give commands. You can have a bossy tone: **Type 8**
- You talk a lot. At times, you tell too much: **Type 9**

What does your room look like? Your room may be an outward display of your Enneagram type.

- Your space is clean and simple. It has a lot of blacks, whites, and grays. You have eco-friendly things: **Type 1**
- Your space is cozy. It has a lot of sentimental things. This includes photos, gifts, and souvenirs: **Type 2**
- Your space is very organized. It has your achievements on display: **Type 3**
- Your space is unique. It has many homemade things. It has a lot of art: **Type 4**
- Your space is sparse. It only has things you need. It's minimalistic: **Type 5**
- Your space is comfortable. It always has food and supplies: **Type 6**
- Your space has a lot of different things. It pops with color. It may have a vision board: **Type 7**
- Your space has the best of everything. It might have a huge television or eye-popping computer setup: **Type 8**
- Your space is peaceful. It has a lot of plants. It may have open space for doing yoga: **Type 9**

Glossary

ancient (AYN-shuhnt) from a time long ago

average (AV-ur-ij) not good or bad; in the middle

challenger (CHAL-inj-ur) a person who questions things

core (KOR) main or dominant

dynamic (dye-NAM-ik) changing as needed

Enneagram (EN-ee-uh-gram) a 9-sided figure used in a personality typing system

enthusiast (en-THOO-zee-ist) a person who has a lot of positive energy

ethic (ETH-ik) behavior based on ideas about what is good or bad

first lady (FURST LAY-dee) wife of a U.S. president

instinct (IN-stingkt) gut feeling

mystic (MIS-tik) a person who practices deep thought or prayer in an effort to seek spiritual knowledge or awakening

psychiatrist (sye-KYE-uh-trist) medical doctor who studies the human mind

rebels (REB-uhlz) people who break rules

reformer (rih-FORM-ur) a person who changes things for the better

symbol (SIM-buhl) a picture or sign that stands for an idea or concept

triads (TRY-adz) groups of 3

tritype (TRY-tipe) the 3 numbers that make up a person's overall personality

wing (WING) related personality type to the core type

Index